Michael Jordan

Additional Titles in the Sports Reports *Series*

Andre Agassi
Star Tennis Player
(0-89490-798-0)

Troy Aikman
Star Quarterback
(0-89490-927-4)

Roberto Alomar
Star Second Baseman
(0-7660-1079-1)

Charles Barkley
Star Forward
(0-89490-655-0)

Jeff Gordon
Star Race Car Driver
(0-7660-1083-X)

Wayne Gretzky
Star Center
(0-89490-930-4)

Ken Griffey, Jr.
Star Outfielder
(0-89490-802-2)

Scott Hamilton
Star Figure Skater
(0-7660-1236-0)

Anfernee Hardaway
Star Guard
(0-7660-1234-4)

Grant Hill
Star Forward
(0-7660-1078-3)

Michael Jordan
Star Guard
(0-89490-482-5)

Shawn Kemp
Star Forward
(0-89490-929-0)

Mario Lemieux
Star Center
(0-89490-932-0)

Karl Malone
Star Forward
(0-89490-931-2)

Dan Marino
Star Quarterback
(0-89490-933-9)

Mark McGwire
Star Home Run Hitter
(0-7660-1329-4)

Mark Messier
Star Center
(0-89490-801-4)

Reggie Miller
Star Guard
(0-7660-1082-1)

Chris Mullin
Star Forward
(0-89490-486-8)

Hakeem Olajuwon
Star Center
(0-89490-803-0)

Shaquille O'Neal
Star Center
(0-89490-656-9)

Scottie Pippen
Star Forward
(0-7660-1080-5)

Cal Ripken, Jr.
Star Shortstop
(0-89490-485-X)

David Robinson
Star Center
(0-89490-483-3)

Barry Sanders
Star Running Back
(0-89490-484-1)

Deion Sanders
Star Athlete
(0-89490-652-6)

Junior Seau
Star Linebacker
(0-89490-800-6)

Emmitt Smith
Star Running Back
(0-89490-653-4)

Frank Thomas
Star First Baseman
(0-89490-659-3)

Thurman Thomas
Star Running Back
(0-89490-445-0)

Chris Webber
Star Forward
(0-89490-799-9)

Tiger Woods
Star Golfer
(0-7660-1081-3)

Steve Young
Star Quarterback
(0-89490-654-2)

Jim Kelly
Star Quarterback
(0-89490-446-9)

Jerry Rice
Star Wide Receiver
(0-89490-928-2)

Michael Jordan

Star Guard

Ron Knapp

Enslow Publishers, Inc.

40 Industrial Road	PO Box 38
Box 398	Aldershot
Berkeley Heights, NJ 07922	Hants GU12 6BP
USA	UK

http://www.enslow.com

Library of Congress Cataloging-in-Publication Data

Knapp, Ron
    Michael Jordan: star guard   / Ron Knapp
      p. cm. — (Sports reports)
    Includes bibliographical references and index.
    ISBN 0-89490-482-5
    1. Jordan, Michael, 1963– —Juvenile literature. 2. Basketball players—
United States—Biography—Juvenile literature. [1. Jordan, Michael, 1963–
2. Basketball players. 3. Afro-Americans—Biography.] I. Title. II. Series.
GV884. J67K63 1994
796.323'092—dc20
[B]   93-43744
                                                                      CIP
                                                                       AC

Printed in the United States of America

10 9 8 7 6 5

To Our Readers: All Internet addresses in this book were active and appropriate when we went to press. Any comments or suggestions can be sent by e-mail to Comments@enslow.com or to the address on the back cover.

Photo Credits: Mitchell Layton, pp.11, 16, 26, 47, 51, 57, 63, 66, 75, 84, 94 ; Amy E. Powers, pp. 19, 62, 71, 81, 88; University of North Carolina, pp. 31, 39.

Cover Photo Credit: Amy E. Powers

Contents

Chapter 1

"From North Carolina..."

All the lights went out in the Chicago Stadium as soon as the visiting team had been introduced. Spotlights swept over the basketball court and the screaming crowd. Above the center of the court shined the huge red face of an angry bull.

"And now," the announcer yelled, "the starting lineup for your world champion Chicago Bulls!" The best-known athlete in the United States waited impatiently on the bench. As always, he would be the last man introduced.

Under his white and black warm-ups, he wore the number 23 in honor of his brother Larry. In school, he had asked for a number that would be about half of 45, Larry's number. Someday he wanted to be half as good as his brother.[1]

Until he became a professional athlete, most basketball players wore short tight pants that

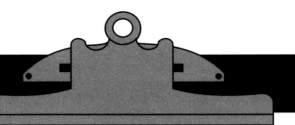

STATS

No NBA player has a better points-per-game average than Michael Jordan. His average after the 1998–1999 season was 31.5, the best of all time.

PLAYER	GAMES PLAYED	POINTS
Michael Jordan	930	31.5
Wilt Chamberlain	1,045	30.1
Elgin Baylor	846	27.4
Shaquille O'Neal	455	27.1
Jerry West	932	27.0
Bob Pettit	792	26.4
George Gervin	791	26.2
Karl Malone	1,110	26.1
Oscar Robertson	1,040	25.7
Dominique Wilkins	1,074	24.8

looked like gym shorts. But when number 23 started wearing baggy pants about two inches longer than the old style, so did thousands of other players in gyms and on playgrounds across the country. Under his Bulls' uniform he still wore blue "North Carolina" shorts. They reminded him of the National Collegiate Athletic Association (NCAA) championship his team won in college.

"From Clemson, a six-ten forward—Horace Grant!" The crowd welcomed Grant with a roar as he ran from the bench through a double line of teammates to the center of the court.

Back on the bench, number 23 was flexing his arms and his shoulders. His upper body was a good deal bigger and stronger than when he played his first game in the National Basketball Association (NBA). In order to go against the huge men blocking his way to the basket, he knew he had to be tough. Working with a fitness expert, he added twenty-eight pounds of muscle to his chest, arms, and shoulders.

Not everyone noticed when he added the upper body strength, but nobody could miss what he did to his head. Number 23 was probably the most recognizable bald-headed man in the world. Every Tuesday and Friday he stood in front of a mirror in his home and shaved his head.

"A six-seven forward, from Central Arkansas—Scottie Pippen!"

Number 23 was still waiting, and for a while his tongue was still safely inside his mouth. During the games, when he went up in the air for a shot, his tongue usually popped out. For years, coaches and trainers tried to get him to shoot with his mouth shut. What if he bumped his chin and bit it? With the Bulls nobody bothered him anymore about his tongue.

Halfway up his left arm he wore a wristband. He'd had one like that since his second year of college. He did it in honor of his friend Buzz Peterson, who had to sit out a season because of a knee injury.[2] His friend's knee healed, but number 23 never stopped wearing the wristband.

"The man in the middle, from San Francisco—Bill Cartwright!"

The packed stadium rocked to cheers for the Bulls' starters standing on the court. But many in the crowd were straining to see number 23 sitting in the dark, still waiting for his turn. They hadn't come to see his baggy shorts or his wristband or watch him make funny faces with his tongue. Ever since he was twelve years old, number 23 had worked ferociously on his basketball skills. That work had paid off. When he played now, he hung

Michael Jordan—the "coolest guy on the planet."

over the court like a helicopter. Larry Bird, one of the game's most talented players, said, "He's God disguised as Michael Jordan."[3]

"A six-two guard, from Notre Dame—John Paxson!"

There was only one player left to be introduced, and everybody in the stadium knew who he was. Michael Jordan was probably the greatest basketball player who has ever lived. He made more money than any other athlete in the world.[4] And beyond his basketball ability and his money, he was, as one magazine put it, "the coolest guy on the planet."[5]

Finally, Michael Jordan was on his feet heading for the court.

"From North Carolina . . ."

Unless you were watching the game on TV, that's all you would hear. The screaming and the cheers were far too loud. In all his years in Chicago, Michael Jordan was never able to hear his name announced.

But there he was at last, on the court with his teammates. He looked down almost shyly. None of the fans were close enough to see the goose bumps on his arms or the tears in his eyes.

As the lights came back on, he always had the same thought. "Even though I can't see many of the people, I think that for some of them this may be the only time they're going to be there. They've never had a ticket before, and they may not have one again, and this is the one night for them."[6]

Jordan slipped out of his warm-ups. He put resin on his hands and shook some of it on the Bulls' TV announcers sitting next to the bench. He walked onto the court and shook hands with the visiting players.

And then, Michael Jordan went to work.

Chapter 2

Country Boy

"The good Lord had a day he just had to do something outstanding. So he created Michael."[1] Years later that was how James Jordan described the birth of his second son on February 17, 1963, in Brooklyn, New York.

Soon after Michael's birth, James and his wife Deloris moved to North Carolina with their baby son and Michael's big brother Larry. The move took the Jordan family from Brooklyn which is part of New York City to Wallace, a tiny town in the southeastern corner of North Carolina. When Michael was seven, the family moved thirty miles farther south to Wilmington, a city of about 40,000 people. Mr. and Mrs. Jordan didn't want their children growing up in a crowded busy city.[2] They wanted Michael to be what he described himself years later, "a country boy from Wilmington, North Carolina."[3]

When he was little, nobody noticed "something outstanding" about Michael. He was just a kid who liked sports. From the time he was two and a half years old, his dad said, "He had a stick in his hand or was bouncing a makeshift ball."[4] He was a well-behaved happy boy.

When Larry and Michael were growing up, their brother Ronald and two sisters, Delores and Roslyn, were born. Both their parents worked. Mrs. Jordan was a teller at a drive-in branch of the United Carolina Bank. After a few years, she was promoted to customer-service supervisor. Mr. Jordan began as a mechanic at a General Electric plant, working his way up to supervisor.

When he was little, Michael picked up the habit of sticking out his tongue when he was concentrating on a job. Michael's father had a workshop in the garage. James Jordan had a habit of sticking out his tongue when he worked with his tools. Michael watched his father and was soon copying him. Whenever the son concentrated on a job, his tongue popped out, too. But Michael never picked up his father's love of tools. "I hate that stuff. I can't do it," he said.[5] His mother agrees. "If you hand him a wrench," she said, "he wouldn't know what to turn

Jordan's famous tongue lets his competitors know he's hard at work.

with it."[6] About the only time Michael picked up a tool as a kid was when he decided to try out his father's axe. He was only five, but at first he did a pretty good job chopping up a few small pieces of wood. But then he missed the wood and sunk the axe into his big toe. The injury healed, and after that he tried to stay away from the tools. Mr. Jordan never forced his son to help in the workshop. "He just pushed me and supported me wherever I chose to go."[7]

Michael was more interested in what his mother was doing inside the house. From her, he learned to cook, sew, and clean. "I was lucky I have parents who care," he said. "They gave me guidance and taught me to work hard. I've learned my lessons."[8]

When he was 7, Michael was playing in the Atlantic Ocean with a friend. "I couldn't swim so we were just fooling around, body surfing and riding the waves," he said. Suddenly a big wave knocked his friend underwater. The boy grabbed Michael to keep from being swept into deeper water. "He needed help, but I couldn't help him because I wasn't a swimmer." The boys were finally separated by the waves. Michael made it back to shore, but his friend drowned. "That's why I don't fool around with water."[9] Even though he went on to become one of the finest athletes in the world,

Jordan never learned to swim. He still hates being in water.

When he was in fifth grade, Michael got a crush on a girl named Angela, who rode his school bus. Every morning he made sure nobody sat next to him so that the seat was saved for Angela. But every morning she would walk past him and sit down next to friends. Even if she had to squeeze in beside two or three other girls, she never wanted to sit by Michael.

He began thinking about ways to make himself more attractive to Angela and the other girls in his class. He noticed that the most popular boys were the athletes. "Why do you think I started to play sports?" he asked. "So girls would like me."[10]

Michael discovered that he was a talented athlete. He played shortstop and pitcher on a Little League Baseball team. "My favorite childhood memory, my greatest accomplishment, was when I got the most valuable player award when my Babe Ruth team won the state baseball championship."[11] He even got his picture on the sports page of the *Wilmington Morning Star*. Mr. and Mrs. Jordan cheered their son's accomplishments on the baseball field. In fact, his dad wondered if someday he might be a major league baseball star.[12]

But Michael found another sport he liked even better. "When he was thirteen," said Mr. Jordan, "I

He's called "Air Jordan" today, but Michael Jordan was nicknamed "Rabbit" when he was a kid.

built a backyard court and he, his brother Larry, and some other kids played almost every day."[13] The boys were on the homemade court for a couple hours after school each weekday, then all day Saturday. "Michael could never walk away from basketball. He'd just play and play and play."[14] The grass in the backyard soon disappeared.

Almost all of the players were bigger and better than Michael. He had to work very hard to keep up with them. He ran and jumped so hard that he earned the nickname "Rabbit." But he could still never beat his brother. "Larry used to beat me all the time and I'd get mad," he said.[15] Michael wasn't winning, but playing over and over against his brother was making him a tougher, better athlete.

He joined the basketball team at D. C. Virgo Junior High School in Wilmington. In his first year, the coaches thought he was just an average player. Soon they realized how hard he was willing to work. He came early to practice and was the last one to go home.

But Michael couldn't play basketball every minute of the day. When he was thirteen, he got a chance to earn some money of his own. His mother had heard about a job at a nearby motel. He waited in the motel office an hour and a half for the manager to come back from lunch. The man must have been impressed by the boy's patience. Michael got the job and was soon spending a few hours a week at the motel. He painted, fixed broken windows, and changed filters in room air conditioners.

The Jordan family wasn't rich, and there was never any money to waste. "I was sixteen when I got my first bicycle," Michael said. "I used to get angry that I didn't have one, but we didn't have a lot of money and I think my parents wanted me to appreciate it when I finally got one. I almost slept with that bicycle when I did."[16]

Like many other teenagers, Michael enjoyed hanging out at the neighborhood mall. He and three of his friends parked their bikes outside, then walked in to watch the shoppers. If they had enough money, they would buy ice cream. Usually, though, they just walked and watched. After a few hours, they rode their bikes home.

Michael got along with almost everybody. But one day when he was in ninth grade, he was dismissed early from school to help prepare the baseball field for a game. He and a friend were supposed to mark the base paths and the foul lines with chalk. While they were working, another teenager walked up to them. He began using racial slurs and hassling the two boys about being out of school.

Years later, Jordan decided that experience might have made him a better player—and a better person. "It was good because it made me know what disappointment felt like. And I knew that I didn't want to have that feeling ever again."[21] He became even more determined.

He played for a year on the junior varsity team. Fred Lynch, one of his coaches, remembers that Michael was very competitive. "He hated losing even then, and that made him work extremely hard when he played."[22] He was the starting point guard and averaged twenty points a game.

That summer he continued to play Larry one-on-one in the backyard. And, of course, his brother was very tough competition. As Michael said years later, "He's got the dunks and some 360s and most all the same stuff I got. And he's five-foot-seven. Larry is my inspiration."[23]

Their father agreed. "I think Michael got so good because Larry used to beat him all the time. He always took losing hard."[24]

During the summer after his sophomore year, two important things happened to Michael Jordan. First, he grew about four and a half inches. Second, he finally started beating Larry in the backyard.

Chapter 3

A Talent Emerges

Michael Jordan was bigger and better as he started his junior basketball season at Laney High School, but he wasn't yet a superstar. As Clifton Herring, the varsity coach, put it, "He wasn't exactly the talk of Wilmington."[1]

While Michael wasn't the best player on the team, he was the hardest worker. Even though he was finally on the varsity team, he went to the junior varsity practice every day from 5 P.M. until 7 P.M. Then he practiced with the varsity for another two hours. On Saturdays and Sundays he was also in the gym. Fred Lynch, by then an assistant varsity coach, said, "Other kids had just as much talent as he did, but they didn't want to pay dues the way Michael did."[2]

Jordan showed what he could do in a tournament game against New Hanover High School. It

The aerial acrobatics of Michael Jordan thrilled audiences in Wilmington.

was a close contest with Laney falling behind in the fourth quarter. Michael got hot and began hitting shots from all over the court. In fact, he scored the Wilmington school's last fifteen points. His final basket was a clutch jump shot at the buzzer that won the game.

That's when the coaches and fans in Wilmington realized Michael Jordan was somebody special. When the games are close and every shot is important, not every player wants the ball. Many players don't like the pressure, but not Michael. When Laney High needed the baskets, he wanted to take the shots. And he usually made them.

But Jordan didn't shoot like everybody else. He lunged; he leaped; he twirled. It was fun to watch him go into the air and see what he was going to do. He didn't look like just another basketball player. He looked like a dancer or an acrobat or a human helicopter (as he would be called later in the NBA).

Michael kept practicing so that he could be even better. In fact, he practiced too much. He wasn't satisfied with being in the gym for four hours after school and then all day on the weekends. He began skipping classes so that he could practice during the school day. When he was caught, he was suspended for a few days. But Michael didn't learn his lesson. When he was allowed back to school, he headed for the gym, not the classroom. He was suspended two more times.

James Jordan was not pleased. He asked his son about his goals. By then Michael had decided he wanted to play big-time college basketball. How can you make it to college, his father asked, if you're not going to graduate from high school? Michael had been concentrating so hard on improving his basketball skills that it hadn't even occurred to him that he might flunk out of school. "I knew he was right and I tried to change," he said. "I concentrated more on my schoolwork. I had a goal and I knew I had to work to reach it."[3]

One of Michael's favorite classes was home economics, which he took for three years. In it, he continued to learn more about skills his mother had begun teaching him when he was a little boy. "I wanted to learn how to do things for myself," he said. He practiced making clothes from patterns. He was able to put together shirts and pants himself. "It wasn't always easy for me, but I did it."[4]

Michael's coaches were impressed now—not just by his ability in basketball, but by his willingness to work hard to achieve his goals. He wanted to become a better player, so he practiced endless hours. He wanted to make it to college, so he attended class and did the work to make it through high school.

Coach Herring believed Michael deserved a chance to test his talent against the best high school players in the country. He contacted the Five-Star Basketball Camp in Pittsburgh, Pennsylvania, and told them about his star. Roy Williams, an assistant coach for the North Carolina basketball team, had seen Michael play and he agreed with Herring. They were able to convince the camp directors that Jordan should be allowed to attend.

So Michael went to Five-Star the summer after his junior year in high school. He was only supposed to be there for a week, and he had to work as a waiter in the lunchroom to pay his way, but at least he was there.

Hardly any of the other players at the camp had heard of the "country boy from Wilmington, North Carolina." But all that changed when they hit the courts. Tom Konchalski, a camp official, watched Michael. "The first time he took a jump shot he got up so high it was like there was no defender. It was like he was playing a different game."[5]

That's the way it went the whole week. Michael was going against some of the best high school players in the nation and he was better than all of them. He won the most valuable player award and four other trophies for his play at the camp. He did so well, in fact, that he was invited back for a second week, during which he won five more trophies.

His stay at Five-Star Camp was a turning point in Jordan's life. He had played his best basketball ever and he had done it against great players. For the first time he had an idea of just how gifted a basketball player he had become. He began to hope that he might get a chance to play at a major college. Several colleges had the same idea. North Carolina State, South Carolina, and North Carolina invited him to attend their schools. Jordan had to make a choice.

When he was young, Michael had hated North Carolina. His favorite college was North Carolina State, where David Thompson—his favorite player—was the star. Thompson and the Wolfpack had won the NCAA Championship in 1974, when Michael was eleven years old and had just become interested in basketball. But his mother, Deloris, was a big fan of the North Carolina Tar Heels. When North Carolina made it to the NCAA title game in 1977, Michael rooted against them. That made his mother mad, but he didn't care. North Carolina State was his team.

Dean Smith, coach of the Tar Heels basketball team, didn't know Michael hated North Carolina.

After Michael began making a name for himself in high school, Smith came to Wilmington to watch him play. Michael was too nervous to talk to the famous coach. He stayed in a corner of the gym, shyly dribbling the ball by himself.

Before making a decision, Michael decided to visit several college campuses. He went to Chapel Hill to see North Carolina and to Raleigh to tour North Carolina State. When he was in South Carolina, school officials tried to impress him by taking him to the governor's mansion. All three schools wanted Jordan on their teams.

Dean Smith, head coach of the North Carolina Tar Heels.

Michael didn't decide right away. He wanted to make sure he was making the right choice. Then, when he was a senior at Laney High, he visited North Carolina again. This time he was a student in a program called Project Uplift. During that visit, nobody on campus knew he was a great basketball star. They just knew he was a high school student on campus as part of a special program designed to encourage minority students to attend the college. Michael liked what he saw at Chapel Hill. The college campus was a beautiful place and he was sure he would get a good education there. He and his parents were also impressed that the school made a special effort to enroll minority students.[6] He finally decided to go to his mother's favorite college—North Carolina.

But Michael still had his senior year to complete at Laney High in Wilmington. And he was still working as hard as ever. Every morning at 6 A.M., Coach Herring picked him up and drove him to school. That gave him an extra couple of hours every morning to work on his game. Then, of course, he still practiced after school and on weekends.

Jordan's hard work continued to pay off. He averaged almost twenty-eight points a game—a very high total for a high school player. He was also taking down about twelve rebounds a game. But Michael was doing a lot more than just compiling impressive statistics; he was putting on a great show. By this time, he had grown another two inches. Now he stood six feet, five inches—tall enough to easily dunk the ball. He began going high in the air close to the backboard and slamming the ball down through the hoop. Sometimes his arm would sweep around like the hand on a clock. Sometimes he would spin his body around in the air before dropping in the dunk. What the fans most enjoyed was watching all the moves he made while hanging in the air before he released the ball. At the same time, of course, his tongue became famous. The wilder the shot, it seemed, the more his tongue stuck out of his mouth. Word was getting around the state of North Carolina that watching Michael Jordan play basketball was a lot of fun.

He finished his last year of basketball at Laney High, graduating in the spring of 1981. Late that summer, he made the 150-mile trip from Wilmington to Chapel Hill to see what kind of a college basketball player he was going to be. He would still wear number 23 on his jersey, but now he would be playing in front of thousands of people in an stadium nicknamed "blue heaven." Today it's known as Dean Smith Stadium.

Having Michael with the Tar Heels for the next few years was going to be like heaven for North Carolina, but nobody was sure of that when he first showed up at the college gym that September. Other players were also there, working out before regular practices began. James Worthy was one of these players. He was the man who everybody expected to be the Tar Heels' big star during the coming season. Geoff Compton, Worthy's seven-foot teammate, was practicing too. So were two former North Carolina stars—Mitch Kupchak and Al Wood, who were by then pros in the NBA.

Jordan joined the pickup game with all those fine players. By then he knew he was good, but he didn't know if he was good enough to be on the court with stars such as Worthy, Compton, Kupchak, and Wood. There was a small crowd in the stadium, and most of them were checking out the new kid from Wilmington.

From the first, Michael played fairly well. As the game went on, his confidence grew. The score was close and finally it was tied. The teams agreed that the next basket would win it. With Wood guarding him, Jordan got the ball. "I drove the baseline and Al went with me. When I made my move to the hoop, Geoff Compton came over to help out. I went up and thought I was trapped. But I just kept going up and dunked over both of them." Jordan's team won. "When I came down, I said to myself, 'Was that really me?'"[7]

Yes, of course, the man making the dunk was really Michael Jordan. And yes, he finally decided he was going to enjoy playing in North Carolina's "blue heaven."

Chapter 4

College Training

When Michael Jordan began his freshman year at North Carolina, nobody knew that he would someday be a pro superstar. Most college players don't make it into the NBA. They have to find a "real" job after they get out of school. One of the reasons Michael chose North Carolina was because he believed it was a great place to get a good education. He made sure to attend all his classes, do his homework, and earn a B average. He was planning to major in geology. Someday, when he was done playing basketball, he figured he might be a geology professor.

Michael's dormitory roommate was Buzz Peterson, a basketball player from Asheville, North Carolina. They had met at the Five-Star Basketball Camp when they were in high school. They became very close friends and spent a lot of time together playing basketball and other sports such as pool and golf. They also double-dated, went bicycling, played games, and studied together.

Buzz noticed one thing about his roommate right away. "Michael doesn't like to lose at anything he does, whether it's cards, pool, or basketball," he said. "There were times when Michael made me stay up all night playing cards or pool, refusing to go to sleep until he was winning again."[1] Once Jordan got so angry when he lost a game of Monopoly that he threw a pile of play money at Peterson.

Another thing Buzz noticed was the closeness of the Jordan family. "What impressed me most about Michael was his love for his parents and family," he said.[2] The friends spent time with each other's families. The Jordans liked Buzz. "We have always looked on Michael's friends as our sons," Mr. Jordan said.[3]

The college teammates spent so much time together that people assumed they were best friends. But Buzz knew this wasn't true. Michael's best friend was always his father, until his death in 1993.[4]

When his freshman basketball season finally began, Michael wasn't sure how much playing time he would get. After all, he was just a freshman, and Dean Smith usually liked to go with more experienced players. But when the coach posted the starting lineup, Michael Jordan was listed as guard.

His starting teammates would be James Worthy and Matt Doherty at forward, Sam Perkins at center, and Jimmy Black at point guard.

There were almost 12,000 people in the stadium for the season opener. Michael had never before played in front of that many spectators. At first he was a little nervous about the TV cameras and the big crowd. When he brought the ball downcourt, it took him a while to decide whether or not to shoot. When he finally decided, the shot missed. But the next time he got the ball he sunk a jump shot for North Carolina's first points. Jordan finished the game with twelve, and the Tar Heels won, 74–67.

Michael seemed to fit in well with Worthy and the other veteran players. Even though he could make the tough shots look easy, he wasn't a show-off. "I'm just a team player who's willing to contribute in any possible way to win."[5] During his freshman season, he went up against many well-known players, but he no longer got nervous. He said playing against fine players just made him want to work harder. Smith enjoyed having him on the team because he was always willing to work hard and listen to advice.

During the 1981–1982 regular season, the Tar Heels lost only two games. Michael was a starter for most of the season and scored an average of 13.5

points per game. Then it was time for the Atlantic Coast Conference postseason tournament. In the closing minutes of play, Michael dropped in four straight jumpers to clinch a 47–45 win over Virginia. He was named to the all-tournament team.

Dick Vitale, the television commentator, was impressed by Jordan's performance against Virginia. "Pound for pound, inch for inch, he's the greatest player in college basketball," he told his audience. Mrs. Jordan was very pleased when she heard about his comments. She gave Vitale a kiss and told him, "Boy I'm so proud of what you said about my son."[6]

Next on the schedule was the NCAA tournament. The Tar Heels kept winning until they earned a spot in the final game against the Georgetown Hoyas—a team that had a spectacular freshman of its own. Patrick Ewing was Georgetown's seven-foot center. The game was played in front of 61,612 fans in the Louisiana Superdome in New Orleans.

In the opening minutes of play, Ewing was awesome—but not very effective. He slapped away the first four North Carolina shots. However, since the ball was coming down when he hit it, each of the four baskets was called good. Because of the goaltending rule, shots can only be blocked when the ball is going up. At the half—despite eighteen points from Worthy—Ewing and Georgetown led, 32–31.

FACT

Each spring the NCAA holds its single-elimination tournament. The team that wins all six of its games is the national champion. North Carolina won the tournament in 1982. The Tar Heels suffered early losses in the tournament during Jordan's last two years on the team. North Carolina State won the title in 1983, followed by Georgetown in 1984.

The game stayed close in the second half. With 3:30 left, Jordan jumped over Ewing and dropped in a shot to put the Tar Heels ahead, 61–58. But then the Georgetown center came back with a jump shot of his own that made the score 61–60. The Hoyas regained the lead with just thirty-two seconds left when Sleepy Floyd's jumper made the score 62–61.

The Tar Heels called a timeout. Many fans expected Coach Smith to order his players to get the ball to Worthy, who already had twenty-eight points. That's what Georgetown coach John Thompson expected. He told the Hoyas to keep Worthy covered. But Smith told the Tar Heels to throw the ball across the court to Michael. As the players walked back onto the court, Smith slapped Jordan on the back and said, "Knock it in, Michael."[7]

The Tar Heels inbounded the ball, and as Smith expected, "Michael's whole side of the court was wide open because they were chasing James."[8] Jordan was about sixteen feet from the basket when Matt Doherty flipped him the ball.

Seventeen seconds were left in the game. Ewing and teammates Larry Spriggs and Gene Smith closed in. Michael went up over them and released a jump shot. Sixty thousand fans held their breath. Jordan said the shot felt good. In fact, it was perfect. The ball didn't even touch the rim as it swished

Dean Smith coached the North Carolina Tar Heels to their first championship game since 1957.

through the net! Michael's clutch shot gave North Carolina a 63–62 lead.

When Georgetown failed to score in the last seconds, North Carolina had its first national championship since 1957. Worthy's fine performance in the tournament, especially his twenty-eight points in the final, earned him most valuable player honors. Michael had sixteen in the title game and was named to the all-tournament team.

But what the North Carolina fans would always remember about the 1982 NCAA title wasn't the scoring statistics or the awards. What they would never forget was the skinny country boy from Wilmington going up in the air and sinking a clutch shot to win the national championship. For a while, Michael was known as "Last Shot" or "Superman" around the Chapel Hill campus. That one basket would change his life. It made him hungry for more big games and more pressure situations. "With that shot it kind of ignited a fire in me that nothing was going to stop."[9]

At first Jordan enjoyed being famous. It was fun to sign autographs. But after a while he became embarrassed when people noticed him or treated him differently because of who he was. When he met people who didn't recognize him, he was careful not to tell them his last name. He wanted them to treat him like just another person.

The Sporting News *named Jordan College Player of the Year after the 1982–83 season.*

Michael still enjoyed the cheers when he was playing basketball, but he knew the crowds in the stadiums didn't really know him. "All these people at the games are here to see me play basketball, not to see me become a better person or get an education. They really don't care about who may give you a job after college or how you do in life."[10] He knew the most important people in his life had to be his family and his friends. And he knew it was up to him to get a good education, and to be a good person and a success in life.

But at the same time he kept working to improve as a basketball player. He had two more great years with Coach Smith at North Carolina. During his sophomore season he averaged twenty points a game and also improved his play on defense. He was so good that Smith allowed him to cover two men at once. He had his own man to cover, but if somebody else close to him got the ball, he was supposed to go after that man, too. Besides his great shots, he also became well-known for his steals.

Jordan made the All-American team after the 1982–1983 season. *The Sporting News* named him College Player of the Year because "He soars through the air, he rebounds, he scores . . . he guards two men at once, he vacuums up loose balls, he blocks shots, he makes steals. Most important, he makes late plays that win games."[11]

He was even tougher his junior season. "He is so much better a player this year, it isn't even funny," Smith said.[12] Bill Foster, Clemson's coach, compared Jordan to Superman when he joked to his players, "Grab his cape and hold on until help arrives."[13] *The New York Times* said, "There are times when he seems too good to be real."[14]

Opposing teams didn't look forward to playing Jordan and the Tar Heels. Guarding him, said Maryland guard Adrian Branch, was "dirty, dirty work."[15] Dan Dakich was the Indiana player assigned to guard Jordan in the 1984 NCAA Tournament. "I remember when I was told I'd be the guy guarding him in that game," he said. "I went back to my dorm room and threw up."[16] Dakich might have been nervous, but he didn't do too badly. He held Jordan to thirteen points, Indiana won the game, and the season was over for North Carolina.

Once again after his junior year, Michael was named College Player of the Year. The Tar Heel Fans began wondering if Michael's college career was over. Would he leave "blue heaven" for the NBA? Many players, such as Worthy, had turned pro before they had graduated from college. Jordan could play one more year at North Carolina if that was what he wanted. He asked Smith for advice. Even though the coach would have loved having him on the team for another year, Smith told Michael it was time for him to turn pro. He was ready for the NBA.

Some fans felt Jordan should stick around for another year to help give the Tar Heels another shot at a national title. The normally easygoing star had no patience with that kind of talk. "I don't owe the fans or alumni a last year at this university," he said. "I have to do what's best for me. If I owe anyone, it's my parents who have put up with me for twenty years."[17]

Michael thought over the advice from Smith and pondered what would be best for him and his family. Finally, he decided to leave the beautiful campus at Chapel Hill and try his luck in the NBA. Money played a big part in his decision. College athletes play for free; NBA stars make millions of dollars. What if he got injured at North Carolina during his senior year and never got a chance to sign a pro contract?

But there was more to the decision than money. "Here was a chance to move up to a higher level," he said.[18] "I feel like it's time for me to move on."[19] Michael Jordan wanted to see how he would do playing against the best basketball players in the world—the superstars of the NBA.

Chapter 5

First Years in Chicago

Hakeem Olajuwon was the first player chosen in the 1984 NBA draft. He went to the Houston Rockets. The second pick belonged to the Portland Trail Blazers. Many fans expected Portland to take Michael Jordan, but instead it chose Sam Bowie—a seven-foot, one-inch center from Kentucky.

Third pick belonged to the Chicago Bulls, who immediately took Jordan. Soon he signed a contract that was worth $6.15 million over the next seven years. Michael agreed that was a lot of money for "a country boy from Wilmington, North Carolina." Of course, it was a lot of money for anybody. It was the biggest contract ever signed by an NBA guard. Michael decided he and his family were going to enjoy the money. He bought a new stereo for his sister and a BMW car for his mother.

But Jordan didn't have a lot of time to relax or

FACT

Each spring the National Basketball Association (NBA) teams divide up the list of college players who want to turn professional. The teams pick one player at a time. Those teams with the worst win-loss records go first. After choosing a player, a team must sign him to a contract before he's officially a part of the team.

to spend more money right away. Before the NBA season began in the fall, he had an extra season of games to play. He had been named to the 1984 Olympic basketball team. The coach was Bobby Knight—the controversial, but highly successful coach at Indiana. He had a reputation for losing his temper, screaming at his players, and being a tough man to play for. But Jordan had no problem. Right away he began working just as hard as he had at Laney High and North Carolina. While waiting for the coach to appear in the gym, the other players rested on the floor and waited. Not Jordan. He always stayed on his feet, dribbling and shooting. He was the kind of player Knight liked.

Besides the United States, the world's best basketball was played in the Union of Soviet Socialist Republics (U.S.S.R.). But in 1984, the U.S.S.R. was boycotting the Olympic games, so the Americans didn't have much competition. With teammates such as Chris Mullin and Patrick Ewing, Jordan and the U.S.A. team ate up the opposition. The Americans destroyed China, 91–49, in the opener. They buried Canada in two games by a combined score of 167–127. The U.S.A. team then hit fifteen shots in a row against Uruguay, whose coach couldn't believe it. "Maybe we have a chance playing seven against five," he said.[1]

Bobby Knight liked Michael's willingness to work and desire to win.

Facing the Americans, Christian Welp, a German player, said, "We knew we were going to lose. We just didn't want to get beat by fifty or sixty."[2] The West Germans did far better than that, losing by only eleven, 78–67. Knight said he was embarrassed by his team's lack of concentration. He worked them harder than ever at the next practice.

But Michael wanted to win and he didn't mind working. Just before the gold-medal game against Spain, he taped a note to the locker room blackboard: "Coach, after everything we've been through, there is no way we're going to lose this game."[3]

Jordan, of course, was right. Spain fell, 96–65, and the Americans got their gold medals. Michael took fourteen shots that game and only missed two of them. He finished the game with twenty points, raising his Olympic average to 17.1 per game. But as usual, the brilliance of his performance went far beyond statistics. Nobody who was in the Los Angeles Forum that August will ever forget the moves Michael put on Spain's Fernando Martin. When he hit the foul line, he was moving. That's when he leapt into the air. Martin tried to go along with him, but he wasn't fast enough to do anything but watch. Jordan spun around in mid-air and slam-dunked the ball with a reverse move over his shoulder!

FACT

Until they lost a 51–50 decision to the Soviet Union in 1972, America's Olympic basketball teams won sixty-three games in a row. Since then, the only other American loss was in 1988, when the U.S.S.R. triumphed again, 76–63. That was the last year the Soviet Union competed in the Olympics. When communism fell in 1991, the country broke apart.

Martin had never seen anybody like Michael Jordan. After the game, all he could say was, "Jump, jump, jump. Very quick. Very fast. Very, very good. Jump, jump, jump."[4]

The Americans, of course, were the class of the Olympic competition; nobody could touch them. The story was very different in Chicago, however. In the two seasons before Jordan arrived, the Bulls had records of 28–54 and 27–55. The team hadn't qualified for a spot in the playoffs since 1981. Chicago fans expected Michael to turn the situation around. It would take time, but within a few years, the fans hoped their team would be one of the powers of the NBA. Jordan told them, "Everyone knows I hate to lose, and I spread that feeling among the team by the way I play. My number-one goal this season is to help make this basketball team into a winner. And I want to have fun."[5]

Jordan made his pro debut for the Bulls against the Washington Bullets. Teammate Orlando Woolridge's twenty-eight points led the Bulls to a 109–93 victory, but hardly anybody noticed. Almost all eyes were on the flashy rookie from North Carolina who scored sixteen points.

Two games later he got thirty-seven points as the Bulls beat the Milwaukee Bucks. Twenty-two of the points came in the fourth quarter. "We couldn't do anything with him," said Milwaukee coach Don Nelson. "We tried double-teaming him, and he just jumped right over it."[6] Then in the ninth game of the season, Jordan had forty-five points as San Antonio fell to Chicago.

Huge crowds came to watch Michael play at the Chicago Stadium and on the road. The fans were dazzled by his moves. Michael Cooper, of the Los Angeles Lakers, was one man who didn't enjoy guarding him. "He goes right, left, over you, around, and under you. He twists, he turns. And you know he's going to get the shot off. You just don't know when and how."[7]

By February 1985, Jordan had played well enough to earn a spot in the NBA All-Star Game as the only rookie starter. He told reporters he would be very nervous playing with all the NBA's big names—people such as Magic Johnson, Larry Bird, Isiah Thomas, and Julius Erving. The All-Star week-end in Indianapolis started out well as he finished second to Dominique Wilkins in the Slam-Dunk Competition. The game itself, however, was a different story. Michael played twenty-two minutes, but only took nine shots. It seemed to him that his teammates were keeping the ball away from him. Maybe they didn't like all the attention the rookie was getting. Maybe they thought he was showing

Michael Jordan's aerial acrobatics mesmerized the crowds
at Chicago Stadium and renewed interest in the Bulls.

off with all his fancy shots and tongue-wagging. "That All-Star Game was the most hurting thing in my whole career," he said.[8]

One of the players he blamed was Thomas, the star guard of the Detroit Pistons. The next time the Bulls played the Pistons, Thomas apologized. Jordan wasn't impressed; he was mad. He said the apology was "for show."[9] That night Chicago beat Detroit in overtime, 139–126. Michael had forty-nine points—his best total of the season. His performance was his answer to the All-Star treatment and to Thomas's apology.

When Jordan's first pro season ended, he had 2,313 points, an average of 28.2 points per game. He also had 534 rebounds and 196 steals. His performance helped improve the Bull's record to 38–44—eleven more victories than the previous season. Chicago even qualified for the playoffs! However, its season was ended by three losses to the Bucks in the opening series. The year had been a satisfying one, and Michael capped it by being named Rookie of the Year.

The Bulls hoped the 1985–1986 season would be more of the same. Late in the opening game, Jordan hit three straight baskets, stretching the Chicago lead to 113–106 over Cleveland. After the Cavs battled back to tie the game, Michael dropped in a

FACT

Each February the best players in the NBA gather for the All-Star Weekend. On Saturday, individual champions are determined for slam-dunking and three-point shooting. On Sunday, the Eastern Conference All-Stars meet the best players in the Western Conference. During his career, Michael Jordan only missed one All-Star Game. That was in 1986 when he was injured.

throw with twenty-three seconds left. The point sealed a 116–115 victory. In the next game, the Bulls came up against the Pistons. The Bulls won, but not before there was a fight, and both coaches were thrown out of the game.

Chicago beat Golden State, 111–105, for its third straight victory. But by the end of the game, Bulls' fans didn't care about the score. Just before halftime, Jordan was headed for a dunk when his foot landed awkwardly and he fell to the court. "It felt like something popped out of place when I came down flat on my foot."[10] He had to be carried to the locker room by teammates Charles Oakley and Mike Smrek. The doctors diagnosed the injury as a severely jammed left ankle. Jordan was on crutches, but he was expected to miss only a few games while his ankle healed.

With its star on the bench, Chicago lost games to the Los Angeles Clippers and the Seattle Super-Sonics. Jordan's teammates said they couldn't wait to have him back. But then the news got worse. On November 5, 1985, a week after the injury, doctors rechecked the ankle and discovered a fractured navicular tarsal bone. One of the bones in his foot had broken when he jammed his ankle. The Bulls' dreams of a great season were gone. The foot would have to be put in a cast so that the bone could heal. Michael would be out of action for several months.

For a competitor like Jordan, it was torture to sit on the bench and do nothing but cheer. Besides, he was afraid the fans and reporters would pay more attention to him than the players on the court.[11] He decided to stay away from the team. To keep busy, he returned to Chapel Hill to take a few classes. He still wanted to get his degree in geology.

In the middle of December, it was time to remove the cast. The Bulls hoped Jordan would be back in the lineup by the end of the month. But X rays showed the bone still hadn't healed. The cast had to stay on for two more weeks. Then it was replaced by a lighter cast so that he could walk on it instead of using crutches. It looked as though he would be able to play early in February.

But then another X ray showed that the foot still wasn't completely healed. A disgusted Jordan again left Chicago for Chapel Hill and more classes. While he was there, he noticed that most of the pain was gone from the foot. He figured it must be healed. Without the knowledge of his doctors or Bulls personnel, he began practicing and playing against some of the college players.

Michael was anxious to get back into NBA action. His team also needed him. During the four and a half months he had been injured, the Bulls had lost forty-three of the sixty-four games they had played. Jordan told team officials what he had been doing in Chapel Hill. Almost everybody was shocked. The doctors, his coach, the owner of the team—even his own attorney—tried to convince him to take it easy. Wouldn't it be better to just sit out the rest of the season and come back fresh for the 1986–1987 season? Michael wouldn't listen. If the Bulls wouldn't let him play, he would just return to Chapel Hill and play there. Finally everybody gave in. Michael was allowed to return to the Bulls' lineup.

In his first game back, he reminded Chicago fans why many people thought he was the most exciting player in the league. Late in the first half, he charged toward the basket. But Randy Breuer—a seven-foot, three-inch center—was standing in his way. No problem: Michael just went up over him and dunked the ball.

At first he played just a few minutes in each game, but by the end of the regular season his playing time was extended to its normal length. When the Bulls once again qualified for the playoffs, Jordan was ready to go. Chicago's opponent was the Boston Celtics. In the first game, Jordan scored forty-nine points, but the Bulls still lost, 123–104.

K. C. Jones, the Boston coach, called Jordan

"awesome." None of his players, he said, wanted to guard the Chicago superstar. "When they saw what Jordan was doing, nobody wanted to go in."[12] Michael didn't care who was guarding him. "I want to win very badly. . . . I want to do the things I couldn't do all season."[13]

That's just what he did in the second game. During most of the action, the four other Bulls on the court stayed near the sidelines or under the net to give Michael plenty of room to do his stuff. By halftime, he had thirty points. The Celtics sent in Kevin McHale to stop him. Michael slipped past McHale and dropped in a reverse dunk. Then it was Danny Ainge's turn. Michael leaped over him on the way to another dunk. With time running out, Jordan had fifty-two points. But Boston still led 116–114. Just before the buzzer rang, Michael launched a three-point shot that missed, but he was fouled by McHale. With no time left, he made both free throws to tie the game and send it into overtime. But even Michael Jordan and the sixty-three points he got that day in double overtime were not enough to stop the Celtics from winning, 135–131.

In the third game, Jordan was held to nineteen points, and Chicago was eliminated from the playoffs, 122–104. But everybody was still talking about his magnificent playoff performance. How

Despite Jordan's high-scoring games, the Bulls were still not championship material.

could he come back from a serious injury and score all those points against one of the best teams in basketball? Jordan said he had only been doing the things his injury had prevented him from doing all season. He wanted to win and he wanted to show the basketball world that he could still play. "When you're out of sight," he said, "people tend to forget you."[14]

Chapter 6

Playoffs, But No Payoffs

The Chicago Bulls started out the 1986–1987 season with a new coach, Doug Collins. The team was trailing the New York Knicks, 90–85, in the season opener when Collins called a timeout. Michael Jordan listened to him for a few seconds, then said simply, "Coach, I'm not going to let you lose your first game."[1] And he didn't. In the fourth quarter he scored twenty-one points as Chicago rallied to a 108–103 victory.

Many of his points that night came on dunks. By then fans had begun talking about "hang time." It seemed to them that Michael could stay up in the air longer than the other players. Sometimes it looked as though he was flying. Against New York, Jordan might not have been flying, but he was jumping very high. It wasn't unusual for him to bang his wrists on the ten-foot rims, but that night he was hitting his elbows! When the game was over, he had fifty points.

A few weeks later, the Bulls and the Knicks were tied, 91–91. With one second left, Michael's jump shot gave Chicago the win. He had forty points in that game, eighteen in a row without missing a shot—an NBA record!

But what most fans remember from Jordan's third season was his performance in the Slam-Dunk Competition in Seattle just before the 1987 All-Star Game. Starting from the opposite end of the court, he charged toward the basket, gaining speed with every step. At the free throw line he went airborne. His arm whipped around twice like a propeller before he crashed the ball through the hoop. The crowd went crazy, and Michael was crowned the king of dunks.

The Pistons weren't very happy to see Jordan and the Bulls on March 4. Another Jordan jumper tied the score late in the game. Detroit's pressure player, Isiah Thomas, took off with the ball for what he hoped would be a game-winning basket. But before he could get off a shot, Jordan stole the ball, sending the game into overtime. The Bulls finally won, 125–120, thanks mainly to Jordan's sixty-one points.

A month later he rewrote the record books by

FACT

In the early days of basketball, there were only two shots, the lay-up and the two-handed set shot. Then came the one-handed shot in the 1930s and the jump shot in the 1950s. All baskets from the floor counted for just two points until the 1960s, when the first three-point lines were painted on courts. Then shortly after that, the dunk became basketball's most exciting shot.

hitting twenty-three consecutive points without a miss against the Atlanta Hawks. That was another sixty-one-point night.

When the regular season was over, Michael had 3,041 points. Nobody except the legendary Wilt Chamberlain had ever scored that many. The Bulls had a mediocre 40–42 record, but again the team qualified for the playoffs. Once again its opponent was the Boston Celtics, and once again the team was beaten. Michael hated to lose, and he was disappointed in his teammates. "They have a tendency to stand around and let me do everything,"[2] he said.

If the Bulls were ever to be a contender for the NBA title, they couldn't be a one-man team. They needed strong players alongside Jordan. For the 1987–1988 season, Chicago took a big step by picking up two fine young forwards, Scottie Pippen and Horace Grant. With returning players such as Jordan and John Paxson, Chicago fans hoped their team was on the way to a championship.

But the star, of course, was still Jordan. On February 3, 1988, the Bulls were facing the reigning champs, the Los Angeles Lakers. Nobody was surprised when the Bulls fell behind, 83–67. And not many people were really surprised by what happened next. Jordan went crazy. He sunk jump shots over Byron Scott and his old college teammate James Worthy. He sizzled past Magic Johnson for a pair of dunks. When he got the ball on a fast break, he sailed by Scott, only to find himself up against Kareem Abdul-Jabbar—the leading scorer in NBA history and one of the toughest centers of all time. Up went Jordan, up went Abdul-Jabbar too, but not high enough. Jordan got the jam. "When Michael took over in the fourth quarter," said Chicago assistant coach John Bach, "it was like a shark in a feeding frenzy."[3] He had twenty-two fourth-quarter points, but the Bulls still lost, 110–101.

On April 3, 1988, Jordan faced Thomas and the Pistons. With ten seconds remaining the game was tied and once again Thomas was on his way to what he hoped would be the game-winning shot. But when he released the ball, Michael knocked it away, took control, and was fouled. Jordan's two free throws won the game, 112–110.

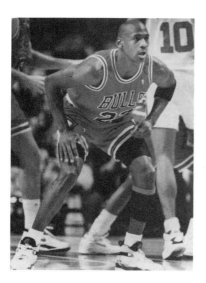

There's more to Jordan's game than just scoring.

With a 50–32 record, the Bulls once again made the playoffs, but this time the team faced the Cleveland Cavs. The Bulls beat the Cavs three games to two. Jordan hit 226 points in those five games. Chicago's game plan was still simple. As Bach explained, "We give the ball to Jordan and say, 'Save us, Michael.'"[4]

But that strategy failed when they ran into Detroit

Not many in the NBA can outjump Michael "Air" Jordan.

in the next round of the playoffs. Each time Jordan touched the ball he was surrounded by three Pistons. Detroit shut down the Chicago offense, and won the series four games to one. Once again Michael was the league's leading scorer. For the first time, he also took most valuable player honors. But once again his team had been knocked out of the playoffs early.

The Bulls had to start all over again in the following season. Michael won his third straight league scoring title. In fact, on January 25, 1989, he scored his 10,000th point in a game against the Philadelphia 76ers. At the end of the regular season, Chicago's record was 47–35. It was time to start the playoffs against the Cleveland Cavaliers.

The teams split the first two games, and then Michael's forty-four points paced a 101–94 Chicago victory. The Bulls led late in Game Four, 99–97, when Jordan stepped up to the free throw line. He missed the shot, and the Cavs got a basket to tie the game and send it into overtime. The match ended in a 108–105 Cleveland victory. Michael knew his missed free throw could have clinched a Bulls' victory. After the game he told his father, "Daddy, I promise you I will never miss in that situation again."[5]

In the final game of the series, Jordan's jump

shot was good with six seconds left, and Chicago led, 99–98. But three seconds later Cleveland's Craig Ehlo got a clutch basket of his own, and the Cavs pulled ahead, 100–99. Everybody in the stadium knew who was going to get the ball, and he did. With time expiring, Michael went up in the air just behind the free throw line. Ehlo was right there with him, so Jordan faked a shot, sailed past the defender, and finally released the ball. It dropped through the hoop to give Chicago a 101–100 win.

Jordan averaged thirty-seven points in the next series against the New York Knicks. In the last game, the score was tied 111–111, with four seconds on the clock and Michael at the line. Both shots were good, so the Bulls won the series and earned a spot in the Eastern Conference title series against Detroit.

Joe Dumars was the Piston who had to cover Jordan. He knew that wouldn't be an easy job. "You make a mistake and you're burned already," he said.[6] But Dumars would have help. Whenever Jordan got the ball, Dennis Rodman and John Salley would join Dumars to triple-team the Chicago star.

Despite the tough Detroit defense, the Bulls won Game One, 94–88. Then after a 100–91 Piston victory, it was once again all up to Jordan. Late in the

With a triple-team defense, Detroit effectively stopped Jordan in the 1989 Eastern Conference Finals.

game, he already had forty-four points, but it was tied, 97–97. Pippen flipped him an inbound pass, and Jordan headed for the basket. Rodman and Thomas were there to stop him, but instead of trying to go over them, he stopped and sunk a short hook shot. The Bulls had a two-to-one lead in the series.

The Pistons' defense tightened in the next two games and the Bulls lost, 86–80 and 94–85. Then Michael hit thirty-two points. But that just wasn't enough. Detroit won the game, 103–94. Another season was over, and the Bulls had to go home again without an NBA title.

Phil Jackson was Chicago's new coach in 1989. But the new season was the same old story. Chicago's regular season record of 55–27 was the team's best in eighteen years. Michael again won the scoring title, and this time when he played in the All-Star Game, teammate Scottie Pippen was there with him.

In the playoffs, the Bulls defeated Milwaukee three games to one. Then the team whipped Philadelphia four out of five games as Jordan averaged forty-three points a game—another NBA record. Then it was time to go against Detroit, the NBA champs, for the Eastern Conference title.

By that time, the Bulls were a much stronger

FACT

When the NBA's 82-game regular season ends in April, the top teams qualify for the playoffs. It's a single-elimination series tournament. After three rounds, only two teams remain—the champs of the Eastern and Western Conferences. These two teams meet for the NBA title.

team than they had been the year before. Besides Jordan and Pippen, Paxson and Grant had also had fine years. Unfortunately for Chicago, the Pistons were ready for them. The defense was tougher than ever.

Jordan managed to score forty-seven points in Game Three and forty-two in the next one. But Detroit still won the series, four games to three.

Michael hated to lose. After dropping two straight Eastern Conference finals to the Pistons, he said, "It's a more serious thing for me, now. That's because I see something I want to achieve so badly."[7] More than the awards and the records, he wanted to play on an NBA championship team.

Chapter 7

The Personal Side

Michael Jordan is almost always a patient and polite man. He signs autographs; he gives money to charity; he makes sure young handicapped people get tickets to Bulls' games; and he gives away his shoes to kids who promise to do well in school. He also visits sick children in hospitals. After most home games, he stops his sports car on a dark dangerous corner to talk with neighborhood boys. Sometimes he invites them to games. Other times he asks to see their grades. Usually they just talk.

Most people don't know about the nice things he does, and that's the way he wants it. "Basketball, all my fans, they have given a lot to me," he said. "This is my way of giving something back. . . . I'll always remember when I wasn't so popular."[1]

That was a long time ago. Today it seems as though everybody knows Michael Jordan. It's almost impossible for him to walk through a mall or eat in a restaurant. As soon as he's recognized—he's surrounded. He can't even visit a barber without causing a small riot! That's why he shaves his head at home. Everywhere he goes, people are watching. "You can feel the eyes . . ." he said. "It's like the eyes are burning into you. It never goes away, not even for one second."[2]

Because of his incredible basketball skill, Michael has lost his privacy. But that same skill has also made him a very wealthy man. He has come a long way from the days back in North Carolina when his family couldn't afford a bicycle for him until he was sixteen.

After the 1988–1989 season, the Bulls gave him a new contract. Over the next eight years he would be paid $25 million. That meant he would earn a little more than $3 million a season. At the time, it was the richest contract ever signed by a basketball player.

By then there was little argument that Jordan was the best player in the NBA, but after a few years he was no longer the highest paid. Patrick Ewing made around $4 million during the 1992–1993 season. In March 1993, Hakeem Olajuwon signed a contract that would pay him even more. Those big paychecks probably didn't bother Jordan much, though, because his basketball earnings were only a small part of his income.

There is little doubt that Jordan is one of the greatest basketball players of all time.

In 1992 it was estimated that Jordan made $32 million from endorsing products. No other athlete earned more than a third of that amount from endorsements.[3] Jordan's first big contract was with Nike. His agent, David Falk, came up with the name "Air Jordan" for a new line of shoes. It was a perfect name because it reminded people of where Michael spends a lot of his time during games.

Shortly before the shoes went on sale, Michael told his friend Buzz Peterson to buy some stock in the Nike company. "They are going to make these Air Jordans," he said, "and someday it's going to be worth a lot of money."[4] Buzz laughed; he thought his friend was joking.

Nike hoped to sell $3 million worth of shoes in three years. Jordan was so popular that sales hit $100 million the first year! By 1993, the total was $200 million annually. If Peterson had taken his friend's advice and bought Nike stock, he, too, would be a rich man today.

Soon, Michael's name appeared on Nike clothing as well as shoes. Wilson Sporting Goods sold a million Michael Jordan basketballs a year. He was the first basketball player to appear on the Wheaties cereal box. He appeared in commercials for Coca-Cola, Gatorade, Chevrolet, Hanes Underwear, and McDonald's. In 1993 there was even a "McJordan Special" hamburger.

FACT

One of the best ways to get attention for a product is to have it endorsed by a popular celebrity. The person is paid to appear in advertisements and commercials. Athletes aren't the only celebrities who endorse products. Entertainers such as Bill Cosby and Cindy Crawford make millions of dollars from endorsements each year.

Together the companies paid Michael $32 million a year because he sold their products. Hundreds of thousands of teenagers and children wanted to wear "Air Jordan" shoes because they thought Michael was "cool." The Gatorade commercials were pretty direct: "I wanna be like Mike" said the song. Millions of people liked Mike, and they were willing to buy the products he advertised.

People liked Jordan because of his talent, and because he seemed like such a nice wholesome person. That's why so many people were surprised in 1991 when a newspaper reported that he had written a check for $57,000 to pay off a gambling debt. The check was written to a man who at one time was convicted of trying to sell cocaine. Michael had lost bets to the man when they played golf and poker. Soon it was revealed he had written checks for another $108,000 to cover other gambling debts. Why was Jordan hanging around with convicts? Why was he betting such huge sums of money?

Jordan admitted he had been wrong. He had been stupid to spend time with a man like that and stupid to have bet so much money. In the future he would try to be a better example to the young people who cheered for him.[5]

Meanwhile, Michael was sharing his financial good fortune with the people closest to him—his

FACT

Michael Jordan's TV appearances aren't just on commercials and in games. In 1991 he was the host of NBC's "Saturday Night Live." "Michael Jordan's Neighborhood," a video for children, was a top-seller. He also starred with Wayne Gretzky and Bo Jackson in "Pro Stars," a Saturday morning cartoon show. In 1992 he appeared in Michael Jackson's "Jam" music video.

family. He formed JUMP (Jordan Universal Marketing and Promotions) to license the use of his name in advertisements. The company also has distributed through the Michael Jordan Foundation hundreds of thousands of dollars to charities such as the Special Olympics and United Negro College Fund. The vice presidents of JUMP are his parents. He also put his brother Larry in charge of a chain of sporting goods stores, called Flight 23, in North Carolina. Several of the stores were managed by his sister Delores.

The Jordan family was also growing. In February 1985, during his first season with the Bulls, Michael was introduced to Juanita Vanoy, an executive secretary with the American Bar Association. After a few dates, he decided "she was exactly what I was looking for."[6] Juanita wasn't so sure; at first she didn't know if they should spend a lot of time together. Could a world-famous athlete really be a good husband? And what about their ages? She was twenty-six when they met, four years older than Michael.

But gradually Juanita fell in love with Michael because, she said, he was such a mature caring person.[7] They were married in September 1989, in Las Vegas, Nevada. Soon they moved into a five-bedroom home in a suburb of Chicago. Their basement is full of weights and training equipment.

The name of Jordan's sporting goods stores, Flight 23, comes from his jersey number.

FACT

Magic Johnson retired from basketball early in the 1991-1992 season after learning he was infected with HIV, the virus which causes AIDS. He returned to the game for the 1992 All-Star Game, the 1992 Summer Olympics as captain of the "Dream Team," and briefly during the 1996 season. Since learning of his illness, he has spent much of his time talking to young people about how they can avoid the disease.

This time Michael didn't cry. He and his teammates celebrated by dancing on the court. Reporters asked if he had any goals left. "I think going for three in a row will give us that challenge we need," he said. "And you have to have challenges to play your best."[17]

The NBA season was over, but there was no time to rest. Michael was to be part of the "Dream Team," the 1992 United States Olympic basketball squad. For the first time, professionals were allowed to play in the games, and so the team had ten of the NBA's finest current players—Jordan, Pippen, Chris Mullin, Charles Barkley, David Robinson, John Stockton, Karl Malone, Patrick Ewing, Larry Bird, and Clyde Drexler. Also joining them was Christian Laettner and Magic Johnson. Johnson was returning after retiring from the sport when he tested positive for the human immunodeficiency virus (HIV) in November 1991.

In Barcelona, Spain, where the Olympics were held, a reporter asked Jordan, "You are so good, are you an extraterrestrial?" Michael laughed and said, "No, I'm from Chicago."[18]

The 1992 American team faced even less competition than had been encountered on the way to the 1984 gold medal. How could anybody expect to beat the Dream Team? The Americans dropped eight opponents by an average margin of 43.8

points per game. In the gold-medal match the team defeated Croatia, 117–85. Magic asked reporters, "When will there be another Olympic team as good as this one? Well, you guys won't be around, and neither will we."[19]

Four months after the Olympics, Juanita gave birth to Jasmine—the Jordans' first daughter. The little girl would become a star when she appeared in the "Michael Jordan's Air Time" video in the spring of 1993. By then, her big brothers, Jeffrey and Marcus, were both playing basketball inside the big Jordan house. In the video, Jasmine, who was just a few weeks old, slept quietly while Jeffrey and Marcus dunked the ball through their miniature hoop.

While "Michael Jordan's Air Time" was a big seller at the videos, the Bulls charged into the playoffs. By then, Michael had been crowned the NBA scoring champ for the seventh season in a row. But Charles Barkley took the 1992–1993 league MVP honors by leading the Phoenix Suns to the team's best finish ever. Barkley figured the Suns had a great chance to stop Chicago from taking its third straight title. In the finals, the Suns managed to win two games, but once again the Bulls were too much. Chicago clinched the series in six games with a 99–98 win.

The summer of 1993 should have been a time for

celebration and relaxation, but in August, police discovered that James Jordan, Michael's father, had been murdered in North Carolina. Two teenagers were arrested for shooting Mr. Jordan as he rested in his car parked on the side of a road. Apparently they had not known their victim was the father of the most famous athlete in the world.

"When James Jordan was murdered," Michael told reporters, "I lost my Dad. I also lost my best friend. I am trying to deal with the overwhelming feelings of loss and grief in a way that would make my Dad proud." He was touched by the response of his fans to the murder. "The many kind words and thoughtful prayers have lifted our spirits through difficult times."[20]

A few weeks later it was time to suit up for the 1993–94 season. Bulls fans were hoping for a fourth straight title. They knew it would be tough. Jordan had said, "Winning a third straight championship was the hardest thing I've ever done on the basketball court."[21] On October 6, 1993, Michael Jordan announced his retirement.

Jordan's retirement was the biggest news in the country. Most fans couldn't believe it, but Jordan had always said he wanted to quit before he began slowing down and losing his skills. "I've always stressed that when I lose the sense of motivation and the sense to prove something as a basketball player, it's time to leave."[22] There was nothing left for him to accomplish on the court.

So what would Jordan do now? He said he was done with basketball. He was not interested in coaching or owning a team. His father had an idea. "He'd make a good politician. Given his fifteen years of popularity, at this rate he could be President."[23]

Instead, Jordan shocked the world and tried out for the Chicago White Sox baseball team. He was assigned to the franchise's Double A team, the Birmingham Barons. He was a competent baseball player; but he was nowhere near a baseball star. Following the 1994–1995 major league baseball player's strike, Jordan decided to return to basketball. To the delight of his fans, Jordan reappeared in the Chicago Bull lineup opposite the Indiana Pacers on March 19, 1995. In just his fifth game back, Jordan scored 55 points against the New York Knicks—a team known for its defense.

At the end of the 1994–1995 season, the Bulls battled it out with the Orlando Magic in the Eastern Conference semifinals. Although Jordan scored 38 points in Game 2 and 40 in Game 3, Orlando won the series knocking Chicago out of the playoffs.

The 1995–1996 season would be a record setting

Michael Jordan, a legend in his own time.

campaign for the Bulls. Chicago enjoyed the winningest season in NBA history finishing at 72–10. Jordan led the league in scoring, pouring in 30.4 points per game, and winning his fourth MVP Award.

The Bulls breezed through the first three rounds of the playoffs by sweeping the Charlotte Hornets, New York Knicks, and the Orlando Magic. The series win against the Magic was especially satisfying because Orlando had beat the Bulls the previous year. In the Finals, the Bulls defeated the Seattle SuperSonics in 6 games. Jordan paced the Bulls with 30.7 points per contest, and was named MVP of the 1996 Finals as well. After the season, Jordan signed a one-year, $25 million contract to stay in Chicago.

The 1996–1997 season was more of the same. Jordan guided the Bulls to a record of 69–13. He led the league in scoring for the ninth time, averaging 29.6 per game. The Bulls cruised through the playoffs once again, winning their fifth championship by defeating the Utah Jazz.

The Bulls rolled through the regular season again in 1997–1998, finishing 62–20. Jordan led the league in scoring and won the MVP award. Jordan led the charge as the Bulls began their playoff stampede. The Bulls ended up facing Utah in the finals for the second straight year. Once again, the Bulls defeated the Jazz in six games. Chicago had won its sixth championship, achieving a second three-peat. Jordan led the league in playoff scoring, and won his sixth NBA Finals MVP award. At that time, the most awards anyone else had won was three.

Jordan retired prior to the start of the strike-shortened 1999 season. He said he wanted to spend more time with his family, and take care of his business interests. No matter what he decides to do, there are many fans that will always consider him to be the best basketball player ever.

Notes by Chapter

Chapter 1

1. Phil Berger with John Rolfe, *Michael Jordan* (Boston: Little Brown and Company, 1992), p. 25.

2. Mitchell Krugel, *Michael Jordan* (New York: St. Martin's Press, 1992), p. 100.

3. ———, "Michael Jordan: The Most Exciting Pro Basketball Player Ever," *Jet*, vol. 80, no. 2 (April 29, 1991), p. 47.

4. Peter Newcomb and Liz Comte, "You want Michael Jordan? You gotta take Boomer Esiason," *Forbes*, vol. 150, no. 12 (February 23, 1992), pp. 96–101.

5. Michael Caruso, "We Like Mike," *Vanity Fair,* vol. 55, no. 2. (February, 1992), pp. 122–123.

6. Bob Greene, *Hang Time: Days and Dreams with Michael Jordan* (New York: Doubleday, 1992), p. 103.

Chapter 2

1. George Castle, "Air to the Throne," *Sport* (January, 1991), p. 29.

2. Bill Gutman, *Michael Jordan* (New York: Archway Paperbacks, 1991), pp. 4–5.

3. Charles Moritz, *Current Biography Yearbook* (New York: H. W. Wilson Company, 1987), p. 290.

4. Castle, p. 30.

5. "Michael Jordan Air Time," CBS Fox Video, 1993.

6. Jim Naughton, *Taking to the Air: The Rise of Michael Jordan* (New York: Warner Books, Inc., 1992), p. 46.

7. "Michael Jordan Air Time."

8. Berger, p. 21.

9. Michael Jordan, *Rare Air: Michael on Michael* (San Francisco: Collins Publishers, 1993), p. 69.

10. Greene, pp. 87–88.

11. Paul J. Deegan, *Michael Jordan: Basketball's Soaring Star* (Minneapolis: Lerner Publications Company, 1988), p. 29.

12. Castle, p. 30.

13. Moritz, p. 290.

14. Barry Jacobs, "High-Flying Michael Jordan Has North Carolina Cruising Toward Another NCAA Title," *People*, vol. 21, issue 11 (March 19, 1984), p. 45.

15. Berger, p. 25.

16. Peter Alfano, "Jordan Settles into Success as a Tar Heel," *New York Times*, p. C6.

17. Greene, pp. 106–107.

18. Deegan, p. 9.

19. Castle, p. 30.

20. Greene, p. 155.

21. Greene, p. 46.

22. Gutman, p. 7.

23. Krugel, p. 11.

24. Gutman, p. 12.

Chapter 3

1. Krugel, p. 14.

2. Berger, p. 30.

3. Berger, p. 27.

4. Gutman, p. 14.

5. Gutman, p. 18.

6. Alfano, p. C6.

7. Krugel, p. 22.

Chapter 4

1. Berger, p. 40.

2. Moritz, p. 291.

3. Krugel, p. 17.

4. Mark Starr, "The Mysterious Death of 'Pops,'" *Newsweek*, vol. 122, no. 8 (August 23, 1993), p. 60.

5. Jacobs, p. 42.

6. "What Michael Means to Us," *Newsweek* special issue, Vol. 122, No. 27, September/November 1993, p. 45.

7. Billy Packer and Roland Lazenby, *The Golden Game* (Dallas: Taylor Publishing Co., 1991), p. 181.

8. Ibid.

9. "Michael Jordan Air Time."

10. Alfano, p. C6.

11. Mortiz, p. 291.

12. Krugel, p. 24.

13. Krugel, pp. 24-25.

14. Alfano, p. C1.

15. Mortiz, p. 291.

16. Krugel, p. 96.

17. Alfano, p. C6.

18. Gutman, p. 60.

19. Krugel, p.36

Chapter 5

1. Curry Kirkpatrick, "Oh, What Men! Ah, What Women," *Sports Illustrated*, vol. 61, no. 9, (August 20, 1984), pp. 73–74.

2. Kirkpatrick, p. 74.

3. Gutman, p. 64.

4. Naughton, p. 84.

5. Krugel, p. 41.

6. Krugel, p. 55.

7. Gutman, p. 75.

8. Berger, p. 66.

9. Naughton, p. 118.

10. Krugel, p. 77.

11. Berger, p. 71.

12. Krugel, p. 85.

13. Berger, p. 82.

14. Gutman, p. 90.

Chapter 6

1. Berger, p. 87.

2. Berger, p. 92.

3. Krugel, p. 159.

4. Krugel, p. 164.

5. Krugel, p. 168.

6. "Michael Jordan's Playground," CBS Fox Video, 1991.

7. Krugel, pp. 172–173.

Chapter 7

1. Deegan, p. 46.

2. Greene, p. 18.

3. Newcomb, p. 101

4. Naughton, p. 85

5. Greene, pp. 357–358.

6. Lynn Norment, "Michael and Juanita Jordan Talk About Love, Marriage and Life After Basketball," *Ebony*, vol. 47, no. 1 (November, 1991), p. 72.

7. Norment, p. 72.

8. Ibid, p. 72.

9. Greene, p. 381.

Chapter 8

1. Packer, p. 228.

2. "Michael Jordan's Playground."

3. Berger, p. 118.

4. Berger, p. 119.

5. Gutman, p. 121.

6. Krugel, p. 181.

7. "Michael Jordan Air Time."

8. Naughton, p. 261.

9. Gutman, p. 129.

10. Gutman, p. 134.

11. Naughton, p. 264.

12. Chip Lovitt, *Michael Jordan* (New York: Scholastic, Inc., 1993), p. 133.

13. "Michael Jordan Air Time."

14. Ibid.

15. Ibid.

16. Ibid.

17. Lovitt, p. 153.

18. Lovitt, p. 159.

19. Jack McCallum, "Dreamy," *Sports Illustrated*, vol. 77, no. 7 (August 17, 1992), p. 16.

20. Associated Press dispatch from Raleigh, North Carolina, August 19, 1993.

21. Jordan, *Rare Air*, p. 103.

22. Leland, John, "Farewell, Michael...and thanks...for the memories", *Newsweek*, special issue.

23. Castle, p. 36.

Career Statistics

NBA									
YEAR	**TEAM**	**GP**	**FG%**	**REB**	**AST**	**STL**	**BLK**	**PTS**	**AVG**
1984–85	Chicago	82	.515	534	481	196	69	2,313	28.2
1985–86	Chicago	18	.457	64	53	37	21	408	22.7
1986–87	Chicago	82	.482	430	377	236	125	3,041	37.1
1987–88	Chicago	82	.535	449	485	259	131	2,868	35.0
1988–89	Chicago	81	.538	652	650	234	65	2,633	32.5
1989–90	Chicago	82	.526	565	519	227	54	2,753	33.6
1990–91	Chicago	82	.539	492	453	223	83	2,580	31.5
1991–92	Chicago	80	.519	511	489	182	75	2,404	30.1
1992–93	Chicago	78	.495	522	428	221	61	2,541	32.6
1993–94	—RETIRED—								
1994–95	Chicago	17	.411	117	90	30	13	457	26.9
1995–96	Chicago	82	.495	543	352	180	42	2,491	30.4
1996–97	Chicago	82	.486	482	352	140	44	2,431	29.6
1997–98	Chicago	82	.465	475	283	141	45	2,357	28.7
TOTALS		930	.505	5,836	5,012	2,306	828	29,277	31.5

GP=Games Played   **FG%**=Field Goal Percentage   **REB**=Rebounds   **AST**=Assists
STL=Steals   **BLK**=Blocked Shots   **PTS**=Points   **AVG**=Points per Game

Where to Write Michael Jordan

Mr. Michael Jordan
c/o Chicago Bulls
United Center
1901 W. Madison Street
Chicago, IL 60612

On the Internet at:

http://www.nba.com/mjretirement/index.htm
http://jordan.sportsline.com

Index